Ellis Island

BY BOB TEMPLE

Published by The Child's World®
1980 Lookout Drive • Mankato, MN 56003-1705
800-599-READ • www.childsworld.com

Acknowledgments
The Child's World®: Mary Berendes, Publishing Director
The Design Lab: Design
Jody Jensen Shaffer: Editing
Red Line Editorial: Photo Research

Photo credits
Shutterstock Images, cover; Library of Congress, 5, 17;
Thinkstock, 6; Underwood & Underwood/Library of Congress,
9, 14; Carol M. Highsmith/Library of Congress, 10; Photos.
com/Thinkstock, 13; Bettmann/Corbis, 18; PhotoDisc_
USLndmks, 21

ISBN 9781623239541
LCCN 2013947300

Printed in the United States of America
Mankato, MN
November, 2013
PA02189

ABOUT THE AUTHOR

Bob Temple is an author and award-winning journalist who has enjoyed a career in newspapers and online journalism. He is also the president of an editorial services and Web content firm based in the Minneapolis-St. Paul area. Bob and his wife, Teri, are the parents of three children. He enjoys traveling and playing golf.

TABLE OF CONTENTS

Gateway to a New Life

For more than 230 years, the United States of America has been a symbol of freedom to the world. In America, people are free to do things such as vote for their leaders, own their own businesses, and choose the churches they want to attend. For these reasons, many people have wanted to move to America to have a better life.

In the late 1800s and early 1900s, more people came to America from other countries than at an other time in our nation's history. Many of these newcomers, called **immigrants**, entered America through Ellis Island. Between 1892 and 1954, more than 20 million immigrants came through Ellis Island. During its peak time, Ellis Island saw more than 1 million immigrants a year.

These immigrants just landed at Ellis Island.

From high above, it is easy to see the many buildings of Ellis Island.

Humble Beginnings

Ellis Island is located just outside of New York City, right next to where the Statue of Liberty stands today. In the 1700s, however, it was called Oyster Island by early settlers in the area, and was later called Gibbet Island. Finally, a man from New York named Samuel Ellis bought the island and named it after himself.

In 1808, the state of New York bought the island from the Ellis family. On the island, Fort Gibson was built to store ammunition during the War of 1812. In the 1800s, immigrants entered New York through a place called Castle Garden. But soon, more immigrants were coming to America than Castle Garden could handle. The government needed a new way, and a new place, to **process** them.

The Island Grows

In 1890, the United States government chose Ellis Island as the site for a new immigration station. At about this same time, the city of New York was digging underground to make its subway system. The dirt and rock dug out for the subway was dumped into the water around Ellis Island. The island grew from about 3 acres (1 hectare) in size to 27.5 acres (11 hectares).

On the island, the government built the new immigration station. It was made up of many buildings, including hospitals for the sick and **dormitories** in which people could sleep. The main building, called the Great Hall, was two stories high. That was the building through which most of the immigrants came. The first floor was a luggage-check area and a ticket office. On the second floor was the registry area, which included the check-in area for immigrants.

Getting Processed

Immigration was exciting, because it brought to America many new people from many different backgrounds. But it also brought some problems. For example, the government had to worry about the new arrivals bringing diseases to the United States.

All passengers on the arriving steamships were given medical examinations while still on the ships. They were also given **vaccinations** to make sure they wouldn't get sick.

Not all of the immigrants who came to America through New York had to go through Ellis Island. Immigrants who had money were often taken right off their ships and brought to New York. Only the poorer passengers were put onto a ferry and brought to Ellis Island for processing.

A Symbol of Freedom

As the **steamships** approached New York and Ellis Island, the soon-to-be Americans were able to see a true symbol of freedom: the Statue of Liberty. The statue was a gift from France to the United States in 1885. Many immigrants would cry when they saw the huge statue. They were happy about the new, better life they were about to find.

Inscribed on the statue are the following words:

Give me your tired, your poor,
Your huddled masses yearning to breathe free,
The wretched refuse of your teeming shore,
Send these, the homeless, tempest-tost to me:
I lift my lamp beside the golden door!

These words mean that America was willing to accept people who were outcasts from other countries. It also meant that people who were not free could find freedom here.

The Statue of Liberty is quite close to Ellis Island.

This picture shows how busy Ellis Island could be.

These immigrants are getting off of the ferry at Ellis Island.
They carry all of their belongings on their way to processing.

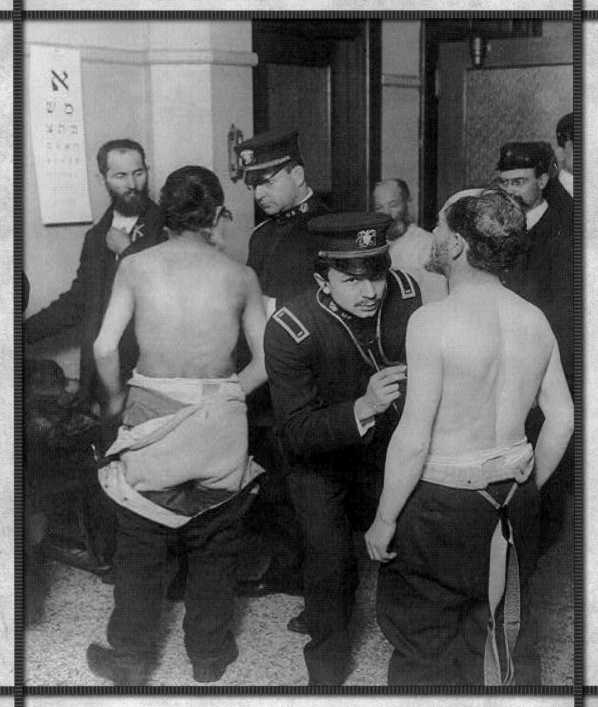

These Jewish immigrants are being examined.

A Scary Experience

Going through Ellis Island was a very scary experience for the immigrants. Many of them couldn't speak English, so they couldn't understand what they were supposed to do. They worried that the Immigration Service would find a reason to send them back to their home countries.

At Ellis Island, medical officers gave the immigrants more physical examinations. In fact, the officers watched the immigrants walk into the building and up the stairs. As the immigrants walked, the officers looked for signs of health problems. They were very concerned about letting ill people into the country. They were afraid the immigrants would make other people sick, too.

Once the immigrants passed their medical exams, they had to answer a series of 29 questions. Usually, an **interpreter** who spoke the immigrant's language helped answer the questions. Most of the questions were easy to answer, such as the person's name, age, the country the person came from, and so on. Almost all the immigrants passed this test, but many had some of their information changed. For example, sometimes a person's name was too difficult for the Ellis Island workers to say or spell. The workers often gave the immigrant a new, shorter name instead.

After the immigrants passed this test, they exchanged their old money for American money. Finally, they were allowed into America!

Some immigrants needed help to answer questions.

This picture shows the new immigration station built after the 1897 fire.

Changes at Ellis Island

Ellis Island had its share of problems over the years. In 1897, a horrible fire burned many of the buildings. It took two and a half years to rebuild with fireproof materials such as brick and concrete.

Corruption was also a problem at Ellis Island. Corrupt workers were willing to let immigrants skip the rules in exchange for money. The corruption decreased after President Theodore Roosevelt ordered it to stop in 1901.

In 1929, a new law forced all immigrants to be inspected at an American office in their **native** country before they came to America. This quickly changed the way immigration was handled in America. There was much less immigration work at Ellis Island. Still, Ellis Island remained open as an immigration station until 1954.

Ellis Island Today

The island was largely abandoned until 1965, when President Lyndon Johnson declared it to be part of the Statue of Liberty National Monument. This action made it a historical site that could be used as a **tourist attraction**. In the 1980s, the Statue of Liberty and Ellis Island were restored.

Today, thousands of visitors go to the island each day and tour the buildings. The Great Hall is now home to the Immigration Museum, where you can learn more about the history of immigration in the United States. If you get a chance, maybe you can visit Ellis Island. Then you can walk through the buildings and feel what it was like to be an immigrant.

The Great Hall has been carefully restored.

Glossary

corruption (kuh-RUP-shun) Corruption is secretly taking money to help someone avoid rules or laws. Corruption was a problem at Ellis Island for a while.

dormitories (DORM-ih-tor-eez) Dormitories are buildings with rooms where people can sleep. Ellis Island had dormitories.

immigrants (IM-uh-grunts) Immigrants are people who move to one country from another. Many immigrants who moved to America came through Ellis Island.

interpreter (in-TUR-pre-tur) An interpreter is a person who translates from one language to another. Interpreters helped immigrants answer questions at Ellis Island.

native (NAY-tiv) A person's native country is where he or she was born. A 1929 law said immigrants had to be inspected in their native countries before coming to America.

process (PRAH-sess) Being processed means going through a series of steps for a certain reason. At Ellis Island, immigrants were processed so they could enter the country.

steamships (STEEM-ships) Steamships are large boats that are powered by steam. Steamships often brought immigrants to America from other countries.

tourist attraction (TOOR-ist uh-TRAK-shun) A tourist attraction is a place many people visit while on vacation. Ellis Island is now a tourist attraction.

vaccinations (vak-sin-AY-shuns) A vaccination is a shot that helps people avoid getting a certain disease. Immigrants were given vaccinations while aboard their ships.

Find Out More

IN THE LIBRARY

Landau, Elaine. *Ellis Island*. New York: Children's Press, 2008.

Levine, Ellen. *If Your Name Was Changed At Ellis Island*. New York: Scholastic, 1994.

Peacock, Louise. *At Ellis Island: A History in Many Voices*. New York: Atheneum Books for Young Readers, 2007.

Thompson, Gare. *We Came Through Ellis Island: The Immigrant Adventures of Emma Markowitz*. Washington, DC: National Geographic Society, 2003.

ON THE WEB

Visit our Web site for lots of links about Ellis Island:
www.childsworld.com/links

Note to Parents, Teachers, and Librarians: We routinely check our Web links to make sure they're safe, active sites—so encourage your readers to check them out!

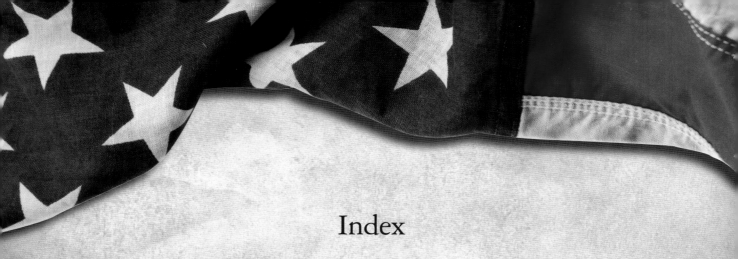

Index